The Supreme Gift

Paulo Coelho

Freely adapts Hernry Drummond's

The Supreme Gift

Translated from Paulo Coelho's Portuguese original by Margaret Jull Costa, 2013.

Original Title: *The Greatest Thing in the World* (Henry Dummond, 1851-1897),
freely adapted by ©Paulo Coelho, 1991
(http://paulocoelhoblog.com/)

Published by:
Sant Jordi Asociados, Agencia Literaria S.L.U.
Passeig de Gràcia, 89 1ª planta
08008 Barcelona
Spain
www.santjordi-asociados.com

Cover design: Mireia Barreras, 2013.
Cover image: Stock.xchng Thiago Ariano.
Author photograph: © Marvin Zilm.
Layout design: Mireia Barreras, 2016.
All rights reserved.

ISBN 978-15-190-0646-2

Do you see this woman? I entered your house; you gave me no water for my feet, but she has wet my feet with her tears and wiped them with her hair. You gave me no kiss, but from the time I came in she has not ceased to kiss my feet. You did not anoint my head with oil, but she has anointed my feet with ointment. Therefore I tell you, her sins, which are many, are forgiven—for she loved much. But he who is forgiven little, loves little.

Luke 7: 44-47

owards the end of the nineteenth century, on a chilly spring after- noon, a group of men and women from different parts of England met together to listen to the most famous preacher of the day, eager to hear what he had to say.

However, having spent eight months trav- elling in various countries of the world, en- gaged in the exhausting work of evangelisa- tion, the preacher felt completely drained and empty. He looked at the small audience, attempted a few phrases, then gave up. The Spirit of God had not touched him that afternoon.

Feeling sad and not knowing quite what to do, he turned to another missionary who was among those present. The young man had recently returned from Africa and might have something interesting to say, and so the preacher asked him to speak in his place.

The people who had gathered in that garden in Kent felt slightly disappointed.

No one knew who this young missionary was. In fact, he wasn't even really a missionary. He had decided not to be ordained as a minister because he had doubts that this was his true vocation.

In search of a reason to live and in search of himself, he had spent two years in deepest Africa, inspired by the example of other people in pursuit of an ideal.

The audience in that garden in Kent were not at all pleased with this change of speaker.

They had gone there in order to hear a wise, famous, experienced preacher, and now they were going to have to listen to a young man who, like them, was still struggling to find himself.

However, Henry Drummond – for that was the missionary's name – had learned something.

He asked someone to lend him a Bible and then he read out a passage from St Paul's Letter to the Corinthians:

If I speak in the tongues of men and of angels, but have not love, I am a noisy gong or a clanging cymbal. And if I have prophetic powers, and understand all mysteries and all knowledge, and if I have all faith, so as to remove mountains, but have not love, I am nothing. If I give away all I have, and if I deliver up my body to be burned, but have not love, I gain nothing.

Love is patient and kind; love does not envy or boast; it is not arrogant or rude. It does not insist on its own way; it is not irritable or resentful; it does not rejoice at wrongdoing, but rejoices with the truth. Love bears all things, believes all things, hopes all things, endures all things.

Love never ends. As for prophecies, they will pass away; as for tongues, they will cease; as for knowledge, it will pass away. For we know in part and we prophesy in part, but when the perfect comes, the partial will pass away. When I was a child, I spoke like a child, I thought like a child, I reasoned like a child. When I became a man, I gave up childish ways. For now we see in a mirror dimly, but then face to face. Now I know in part; then I shall know fully, even as I have been fully known.

So now faith, hope, and love abide, these three; but the greatest of these is love.

veryone listened in respectful silence, but they still felt disappointed. Most of them knew the passage well and had already meditated upon it long and hard.

The young man might at least have chosen something more original, more exciting.

When he finished reading, Henry closed the Bible, looked up at the sky and began to speak.

All of us, at some point, have asked the same question that every generation asks: What is the most important thing in life?

We want to use our days well, because no one else can live our lives for us. So we need to know where we should focus our efforts, what our supreme goal in life should be?

We are used to being told that the greatest treasure in the spiritual world is Faith. Many centuries of religion rest on that one simple word.

Do we consider Faith to be the most important thing in the world? If so, we are quite wrong.

If we do, at some point, believe that, then we might as well stop believing.

The passage I have just read out takes us back to the early days of Christianity. And as we heard: 'So now faith, hope, and love abide, these three; but the greatest of these is love.'

This is no superficial judgement on the part of Paul, who wrote these words. After all,

a moment before, he was speaking about Faith.
He said: 'If I have all faith, so as to remove
mountains, but have not love, I am nothing.'

Paul does not avoid the subject, on the contrary, he compares Faith and Love and con-
cludes:

'...and the greatest of these is Love.'

It must have been very hard for him to say
that; after all, we usually commend to others
what we consider to be our own strongest point,
and love was not Paul's strong point. Any ob-
servant student will have noticed that, as he
grew older, Paul became more tolerant, more
tender-hearted. However, the hand that wrote
'the greatest of these is Love' had often been
stained with blood in its youth.

Besides, this Letter to the Corinthians is
not the only document to state that Love is the
summum bonum, the highest or supreme good.
All the major works in Christianity agree on
that point.

Peter says: 'Above all, hold unfailing your

love for one another, since love covers a multitude of sins.'

John goes still further: 'God is Love.'

In another text of Paul's, we read: 'Love is the fulfilling of the Law.'

Why did Paul say that? At the time, people thought that the way to reach Paradise was by keeping the Ten Commandments, as well as the hundreds of other commandments based on the Tablets of the Law. Fulfilling the law was everything. It was more important than life itself.

Then Christ said: 'I will show you a simpler way. If you do one thing, you will do these hundred and ten things, without ever thinking about them. If you love, you will unconsciously fulfill the whole law.'

We can judge for ourselves if this advice works. Take any one of the commandments:

'Thou shalt have no other gods before Me.' That is Love.

'Take not His name in vain.'

Would we dare to speak lightly of someone

we love? 'Remember the Sabbath day to keep it holy.'

Do we not wait longingly for the day when we will meet our beloved in order to devote ourselves to Love? It will be the same if we love God.

Love requires us to obey all of God's laws.

When someone loves, there is no need to tell him that he must honour his father and his mother or that he must not kill. It would be offensive to tell anyone who loves his fellow man and woman that he must not steal – how could he steal from those he loves? And why urge him not to bear false witness? He would never do such a thing, just as he would be utterly incapable of coveting his neighbour's wife.

Love, then, is 'the fulfilling of the Law'.

Love is the rule that contains all the other rules.

Love is the commandment that justifies all the other commandments. Love is the secret of life.

Paul learned this and, in the letter I read from just now, he gave us the best and most important description of the *summum bonum* – the highest good.

**P**aul begins by comparing Love with other qualities that were greatly valued at the time. He compares it with eloquence; a noble gift capable of touching people's hearts and minds and encouraging them to carry out important sacred tasks or deeds that go above and beyond the call of duty.

Paul says of great preachers: If I speak in the tongues of men and of angels but have not love, I am become a noisy gong, or a clanging cymbal.

And we all know why. We often hear what seem to be great ideas capable of transforming the world. But they are mere words devoid of emotion, empty of Love, which is why they do not touch us, however logical and intelligent they may seem.

Paul compares Love with Prophecy. He compares it with Mysteries. He compares it with Faith. He compares it with Charity.

Why is Love greater than Faith?

Because Faith is merely a path that leads us to the Greater Love. Why is Love greater than Charity?

Because Charity is merely one of the ways in which Love manifests itself. And the whole is always greater than its individual parts. Charity is also merely a path, one of the many paths that Love uses to bring us closer to our fellow man.

And, as we all know, there is also a kind of Charity in which Love plays no part. It's so easy to toss a coin to a poor man in the street; in fact it's usually easier to do that than not.

It frees us from the guilty feelings aroused by the cruel spectacle of poverty.

What a relief, and purchased with just one coin! It's cheap for us and solves the beggar's problem.

However, if we really loved that poor man, we would do far more for him.

Or perhaps less. We would not toss him a coin and, who knows, our guilty feelings might arouse real Love in us.

P aul then compares Love with sacrifice and martyrdom. And I say to those who hope one day to work for the good of humanity: *If I deliver up my body to be burned, but have not love, I gain nothing.* Nothing!

You cannot give anything more important than the Love reflected in your own life. That is the one true universal language, which allows us to speak Chinese or the dialects of India. For if, one day, you go to those places, the silent eloquence of Love will mean that you will be understood by everyone.

A man's message of Faith lies in the way he lives his life and not in the words he says.

Not long ago, I was in the heart of Africa, near the Great Lakes. There I met men and women who remembered with affection the one white man they had encountered: David Livingstone. And while I followed his footsteps through the Dark Continent, people's faces lit up as they told me about the doctor who had passed through there some three years before. They could not understand what Livingstone said to them, but they felt the Love that was there in his heart.

Take that same Love with you and the work you do will be fully justified.

When you speak about God and the world of the spirit, there can be no more eloquent subject. There is no point in talking about miracles, witnesses of Faith, fine prayers. If you do all that but have not Love, all your efforts will be in vain.

You may accomplish everything you set out to accomplish and be prepared to make any sacrifice, but if you give your body to be burned and have not Love, you will have achieved nothing for yourself or for God's cause.

fter comparing Love with all those things, Paul – in three short verses – gives an amazing analysis of that Greatest of Gifts.

He tells us that Love is made up of many things.

Like light. We learn at school that if we pick up a prism and allow a ray of light to pass through it, that ray will divide up into seven colours.

The colours of the rainbow.

Then Paul takes Love and allows it to pass

through the prism of his intellect, dividing it up into its various elements.

He shows us the rainbow of Love, just as a prism reveals to us the rainbow colours of light.

And what are those elements? They are virtues we hear about every day and that we can practise at every moment in our lives.

It is these small things, these simple virtues, that make up the Supreme Gift of Love.

L ove is made up of nine in- gredients:

Patience: *Love is patient...*

Kindness: *...and kind.*

Generosity: *Love does not envy...*

Humility: *...or boast; it is not arrogant...*

Courtesy: *...or rude.*

Unselfishness: *It does not insist on its own way.*

Good temper: *It is not irritable... or resentful.*

Guilelessness: *or resentful.*

Sincerity: *It does not rejoice at wrongdoing, but rejoices with the truth.*

Patience. Kindness. Generosity. Humility. Courtesy. Unselfishness. Good temper. Guilelessness. Sincerity. All these things make up the Supreme Gift, and are there in the soul of whoever wishes to be in the world and close to God.

All these gifts are to do with us, with our daily lives, with today and tomorrow, not with eternity.

We hear a lot about loving God.

But Christ talks to us about loving our fellow man. We seek peace in Heaven.

Christ seeks peace on Earth.

Our human search for the answer to our main question - What should I do with my life? - is not some strange thing imposed on us from outside.

It is to be found in all civilisations, because it was born along with mankind and is evidence of the breath of the Eternal Spirit in the world.

The Supreme Gift reflects that breath. It is not just a Gift in itself, but the words and acts that make up the sum of every ordinary day.

L ove is **patience**. That is how Love normally behaves: it waits calmly, unhurriedly, knowing that at some point, it will show itself.

Love is ready to do its work at the right moment, but it waits calmly and meekly. Love is patient. It can bear all things.

It believes all things. It hopes for all things. Because Love understands.

**indness**. Active love. Have you ever noticed how much of Christ's time in the world was spent doing kind deeds, how large a part of his short time on Earth was spent merely making other people happy.

If you view his life in that way, you will notice that although Christ had much to do, he never forgot to be kind to his fellow man.

There is only one thing greater than happiness, and that is holiness. That may not be within our grasp, but making other people happy is. God gave us that ability and it costs us almost nothing. When you think about it, you will see that it costs us absolutely nothing.

So why are we so reluctant to make our fellow man happy? Happiness does not breed in captivity nor does it diminish when it is given away. On the contrary, merely by sowing happiness, we increase our quota. Someone once said: 'The greatest thing a man can do for his Heavenly Father is to be kind to some of His other children.'

The world really needs that!

And it's so easy to be kind. The effect is immediate and you will be remembered for ever.

And the reward is abundant, for no debt is more honoured than the debt of Love. 'Love never ends.'

Love is the true energy of life. As Browning says:

For life, with all it yields of joy and woe.
And hope and fear — ...

Is just our chance o' the prize of learning love,

How love might be, hath been indeed, and is...

***

Where Love is, so are we, and so is God.

Anyone who takes joy in Love, takes joy in their existence as a human being, takes joy in God.

God is Love. Therefore love!

Without distinction, without calculation, without procrastination, without fear that you might suffer: love!

Lavish your Love on the poor, which is easy, and on the rich, who distrust everyone and cannot recognise the Love they need so much; and on your equals, which is very difficult. It is with our equals that we are at our most selfish. We often try to please, but what we need to do is to give pleasure.

Give pleasure. Never miss an opportunity to give pleasure, because you will be the first to benefit from that – even if no one knows what you are doing. The world around you will become more contented and things will be easier for you. As Stephen Grellet wrote: 'I shall pass through this world but once. Any good therefore that I can do or any kindness that I can show to any human being, let me do it now. Let me not defer or neglect it, for I shall not pass this way again.'

**G**enerosity: 'Love does not envy.' Envy means love in competition with the Love of others. Let others love. And try to love still more. Do your part, do your best.

Whenever you want to do a good deed, you will find other people doing the same thing, sometimes much better than you. Do not envy them.

Envy is directed at those in the same line of work as ourselves, and is generally intent on destroying what is best in them. It is the most despicable of all human feelings.

Envy is always waiting to destroy everything that other people do, even if they do it better than we do.

And the only way to escape envy is to focus all your energies on Love.

Instead of envying, we should admire the large, rich, generous soul that does not envy.

nd having learned all that, we must learn something else: **humility**. Place a seal on your lips and forget your patience, your kindness, your generosity. Once Love has entered your life and done its beautiful work, sit quietly and say nothing about it.

Love hides even from itself.

Love avoids even self-satisfaction. Love does not boast; it is not arrogant.

T he fifth ingredient is something that might seem strange and pointless in this rainbow of Love: **courtesy**. This is Love among people, Love in society. A lot of people say that courtesy is a superfluous feeling.

Not true. Courtesy is Love in little things.

'Love is not rude.' You might be the shyest person in the world, the least well prepared for dealing with others, but if you have a reservoir of Love in your heart, you will always behave correctly.

Carlyle said of Robert Burns that there was no truer gentleman in Europe than the ploughman poet, because he loved everything – the mouse, the daisy, and all God's creatures great and small. This meant that Burns could speak to anyone, and visit courts and palaces from his own modest little cottage.

Do you know the meaning of the word 'gentleman'? It means someone who does things gently. That is the whole art and mystery of Love.

Someone who has Love in his heart cannot act in an ungentlemanly manner, whereas the false gentleman, who is merely a snob, is a prisoner of his feelings and cannot love.

'Love is not rude.'

Unselfishness. 'Love does not insist on its own way.' Love does not even seek what is hers by right.

In England, as in many other countries, men struggle – and justly so – for their rights. But there are certain moments when we can give up those rights.

Paul, however, does not demand this of us, because he knows that Love is something so profound that no one who loves does so thinking of a reward.

One loves because Love is the Greatest Gift, not because it gives us something in return.

It isn't hard to give up our rights; after all, they are outside us, bound up in our relationship with society. What is hard is to give up ourselves. It is still harder to seek nothing for ourselves at all.

Generally speaking, in seeking, buying, winning and deserving those things, we have had the best of them already, and we can, in a noble gesture, forego any reward. But I am talking about not seeking at all.

Id opus est. That is the task. Love is sufficient unto itself.

'And do you seek great things for yourself?' asks the prophet. 'Seek them not.' Why? Because there is no greatness in things. Things cannot be great. The only greatness is unselfish Love.

I know that it is hard to give up a reward, but it is much harder to seek no reward at all.

No, I shouldn't say that. Nothing is too difficult for Love. I believe that the burden of

Love is light. The 'burden' is merely Love's way of living. And I am sure that it is also the easiest way to live, because the Love that seeks no reward can fill every minute of existence with its light.

The lesson to be found in all spiritual teachings is that there is no happiness in having and getting, only in giving.

I repeat: **There is no happiness in having and getting, only in giving**.

Almost everyone nowadays is on the wrong track in their pursuit of happiness. They think a great deal about having and receiving, about outward show and success and being served by others. That is what most people call fulfillment.

True fulfillment, though, lies in giving and serving. 'Whoever would be first among you,' said Christ, 'must be the slave of all.' He that would be happy should place Love above all else in life. Nothing else matters.

T he next ingredient is **good temper.** Love 'is not provoked'.

We are inclined to view bad temper as a family failing, a personality trait, a matter of temperament, when we should really see it as a character defect. That is why, in his analysis of Love, Paul makes a point of mentioning good temper. And there are many other Biblical passages that cite bad temper as the most destructive element in human nature.

What surprises me is that bad temper is often there in the lives of people who consider themselves to be virtuous, and can be a great blot on an otherwise noble, gentle nature. We know a lot of people who are almost perfect, but then, suddenly, they decide that they are right about something and lose their temper.

The supposed compatibility of virtue and bad temper is one of the saddest problems afflicting humanity and society.

There are, in fact, two kinds of sin: sins of the body and sins of the disposition. In a parable in the New Testament, the Prodigal Son abandons his family and goes off into the world, while the elder brother stays with the father. After many misfortunes, the Prodigal Son decides to return, and the father gives a great party in his honour. When the brother finds out, he angrily asks his father: 'Did I not stay here by your side all this time, working, while he was squandering his inheritance?'

The Prodigal Son can be seen as committing the first kind of sin, while his brother commits the second. Curiously, society has no doubt as to which of those two kinds of sin is worse, and condemnation falls, unchallenged, on the Prodigal Son. But are we right?

We do not have a balance in which to weigh one another's sins, and 'better' or 'worse' are only words in our vocabulary. But I would say to you: more sophisticated faults can be far more serious than simpler and more obvious ones.

In the eyes of Him who is Love, a sin against Love is a hundred times worse. No vice, be it desire, avarice, lust or drunkenness, is worse than an evil temper.

When it comes to embittering lives,

destroying communities,

breaking up relationships,

devastating homes,

withering up men and women,

taking the bloom off youth,

for sheer gratuitous, misery-producing power,

ill temper has no rival.

Look at the elder brother: very proper, hard-working, patient, responsible, and all credit to him for his virtues. Then look at this boy, this child, sulking outside his own father's door.

'He was angry,' we read, 'and refused to go in.' Think of the effect his brother's attitude must have had on the Prodigal Son! And how many prodigal sons are kept out of the Kingdom of God by the loveless people who profess to be inside!

Imagine the face of the elder brother as he says those words, from underneath a cloud of jealousy, rage, pride, cruelty, self-righteousness, stubbornness, resentment and a lack of charity. Those are the ingredients of that dark, loveless soul. Those are the ingredients of bad temper and intolerance.

And any of us who have experienced such pressures in life know that these sins are far more destructive than the sins of the body.

Did not Christ say that the publicans and

the harlots would enter the Kingdom of Heaven ahead of the scholars of the day?

There is no place in the Kingdom for the ill-tempered and intolerant. One such man would make Paradise unbearable for everyone else.

Unless he be born again, and leave aside everything he considers untouchable and certain, he cannot, simply cannot, enter the Kingdom of Heaven, because in order to enter the Kingdom of Heaven, he must carry Paradise in his soul.

nd yet, as you see, even while I was speaking, I began to grow angry. A bubble of irritation rose up, revealing some rottenness underneath. That is the great test of Love: knowing that, however hard we try, we almost never achieve the necessary peace for Love to flourish. See how the most hidden parts of the soul surface as soon as we lower our guard. And so, suddenly, while preaching generosity, humility, patience, courtesy and unselfishness, temper flared.

I fell into the vice of all those who speak of virtue: intolerance.

You see, it is not enough merely to speak of these ideas or to struggle with them. We have to seek out their hiding place, to change our innermost nature. Then all feelings of anger will die of their own accord. Then our souls will grow gentler, not because we took out aggression, but because we put in Love.

God is Love, a Love which, as it penetrates us, sweetens, purifies and transforms everything. It drives out all error, it renews, regenerates and rebuilds the inner man.

Will-power alone cannot transform you. Love can.

Therefore, let Love in. Remember: this is a matter of life and death. There is no point my standing here and talking about Love if I am incapable of Love myself. 'Whoever causes one of these little ones who believe in me to sin, it would be better for him to have a great millstone fastened around his neck and to be drowned in the depth of the sea.'

That is to say, it is better not to live than not to love.

It is better not to live than not to love.

L et us speak a little about **guilelessness and sincerity**. The people who influence and touch us most deeply are those who believe what we say.

Suspicion makes people shrivel up.

Faced by guilelessness, however, we grow and expand. We find courage and friendship beside those who believe in us.

Those who understand us can transform us.

It is good to know that there are still people who think no evil, because they know the importance of the good they are doing. Those people grow in the eyes of men and of God. They are unafraid of envy or indifference because Love 'thinketh no evil', always looks on the bright side, always looks for the positive in every action.

And again, he who loves wins, even though he sought no reward. How marvellous to live always in the light! What a stimulus, what a blessing to spend an entire day without once thinking evil!

To be trusted is to be very close to Love. And we will only achieve that if we trust in other people. The little harm that others can do us because of our guilelessness is as nothing compared to our joy in the face of life. There will no longer be any need to wear heavy armour, bulky shields and dangerous weapons. Guilelessness will protect us.

We can only help someone if we trust him. If we respect others, we will recover our self-respect.

If we believe that someone can improve and that person feels we consider him to be our equal, he will hear our words and believe he can be a better person.

 L ove 'does not rejoice at wrongdoing, but rejoices with the truth'. I called this ingredient **sincerity**.

He who loves will love Truth as much as he loves his fellow man. He will rejoice in the Truth, but not in what he was taught to believe.

Not in the truth of doctrines.

Not in the truth of churches.

Not in this 'ism' or that 'ism'.

He will rejoice in the *Truth*. He will seek

the Truth with a humble, unbiased mind and will be contented with what he finds.

Perhaps the word *sincerity* is not the best one to describe that quality of Love, but I cannot come up with a better one.

I am not talking about the kind of sincerity that humiliates someone else, that pounces on other people's mistakes in order to show how good we are. Real Love does not consist in exposing other people's weaknesses, but in accepting everything and rejoicing to see that things are better than people said they were.

 o much for the analysis of Love. Now we have to try and fit all those ingredients into our characters.

That should be our objective in the world: learning to love.

Life offers us endless opportunities to learn how to love. Every man and every woman, every day of their lives, has ample opportunity to give themselves to Love. Life is not a holiday, but an education.

And the most important lesson we can learn is how to love.

How to love better.

What makes someone a great artist, a great writer or a great musician?

Practice.

What makes someone a great man or woman?

Practice. Nothing else.

Spiritual growth applies the same laws used by body and soul. If you don't exercise your arms, you will never develop your biceps. If you don't exercise your soul, you will never develop strength of character or beauty of spiritual growth.

Love is not a brief moment of enthusiasm.

Love is the rich, strong, generous expression of our being – character in its fullest sense. And to build that requires constant practice.

What was Christ doing in the carpenter's workshop?

Practising.

Even though he was perfect, we read that

he learned obedience and thus grew in wisdom and in favour with God and men.

Try to see the world as a great education in Love and do not quarrel with your lot in life. Do not complain because of your unending cares and anxieties, your mean surroundings, the small and sordid souls you are obliged to live with.

That is God's way of making you **practise**.

And do not be alarmed by temptation or surprised because it is always there and never moves away, despite all your efforts and prayers. That is God's way of putting your soul to work.

All these things are teaching you to be patient, humble, generous, unselfish, kind and courteous. Do not push away the Hand that is shaping your image, because that Hand is also showing you your path.

Be assured, you are growing more beautiful with each minute that passes – and although it may not seem like it, difficulties and temptations are God's tools.

Remember Goethe's words: '*Talent develops itself in solitude; character in the stream of life.*'

Talent develops itself in solitude, through prayer, faith, meditation and seeing the unseen.

But character can only grow if we remain in the stream of life. Because it is in the world that we learn to love.

 **I** have named a few of the elements of Love as a way of helping us understand God and our fellow man. However, these are only elements. Love can never be defined.

Light is more than the sum of its ingredients – it is something that glows and shines in space.

And Love is much more than the sum of all its ingredients – it is something living, pulsating, divine.

If we were to mix together all the colours of the rainbow, we would simply create the colour white - not light.

In the same way, if we put together all the virtues we have talked about, we might become virtuous, but that doesn't mean we would have learned to love.

So how do we go about bringing Love into our hearts?

We work our will hard in order to keep Love close.

We try to copy those who have learned to love.

We forget all the rules telling us what Love is, including everything I have said here.

We pray.

We watch.

N one of that, however, will make us love, because Love is an **effect**. And only when we know the cause will the effect be produced.

Shall I tell you what that cause is?

When we read the Revised Version of the First Epistle of John, we find these words:

'We love because He first loved us.'

That is what is written: 'we love' not 'we

love Him', as it appeared in the earlier King James version.

'We love because He first loved us.' Notice that word **because**.

That is the cause I mentioned.

Because He first loved us, the effect – the consequence – is that we love too. We are all manifestations of Love.

We love Him, we love ourselves, we love everyone.

That is how it is. Our heart is slowly transformed. Consider the Love that is given to you and you will know how to love.

You cannot force yourself – or anyone else – to love. All you can do is look at Love, fall in love with it and copy it.

Love love. Remember the great sacrifice He made and, by loving Him, you will become like Him.

Love begets Love.

If you place a piece of iron close to a source of electricity it will, by a process of induction, become electrified. If you place it close to a magnet, it will become a magnet for as long as the other magnet is there.

Remain close to Him who loved us and you will be magnetised by that Love. Anyone who seeks the cause will feel the effect.

Try to free yourself from the idea that the spiritual search exists purely by chance or by caprice or because of our liking for mystery. It is there because of a natural or, rather, spiritual law, because it is a divine law.

Edward Irving went to visit a dying boy. When he entered the room, he placed his hand on the boy's head and said: 'My boy, God loves you.'

And he said nothing more. He just went away.

The boy got out of bed and called to all the people in the house: 'God loves me! God loves me!' The change was extraordinary; the certainty that God loved him gave him strength and destroyed whatever was wrong with him and began his transformation.

In the same way, Love melts any ill or evil in a man's heart and transforms him into a new creature, patient, humble, generous, gentle, unselfish and sincere.

There is no other way of loving, nor is there any mystery to it. We love others, we love ourselves, we love our enemies, because He first loved us.

T here is little more to add about Paul's reasons for considering Love to be the Greatest Gift, except to analyse the most important reason, which can be summed up very briefly:

Love never ends.

'*Love*,' Paul insists, '*never ends.*' Then he gives us another of his marvellous lists. He speaks of matters that were important in his day, things that everyone thought would last, and he shows all of them to be fleeting, temporary, passing away.

'As for prophecies, they will pass away.'

At the time, every mother's dream was for her son to become a prophet. For hundreds of years, God had chosen to speak to the world through prophets and they were more powerful than kings. Men waited anxiously for a new messenger from on High to arrive and then hung on his every word.

Paul is implacable: *'As for prophecies, they will pass away.'*

The Bible is full of prophecies, but once they were fulfilled, they lost their meaning. They disappeared as prophecies and remained only to feed the faith of devout men.

Then Paul speaks about languages:

'As for tongues, they will cease.'

As far as we know, thousands of years have passed since languages first appeared on the face of the Earth. They helped man to survive in a dangerous, hostile world. Where are those languages? They disappeared.

The Egyptians built pyramids and carved their writing on monuments that are still there today. The Egyptians continue to exist as a nation, but their original language has disappeared.

Take these examples in any sense you like, even in the literal sense.

Although it was not Paul's main concern, it can at least help us to understand what he meant. The Letter to the Corinthians, which we have been reading and discussing, was written originally in ancient Greek.

If we went to Greece with the original text, very few people would be able to decipher it.

1,500 years ago, Latin dominated the world, that domination has long since ceased. Look at indigenous languages: they are fast disappearing. The original languages of Wales and Scotland are dying before our eyes.

The most popular book in England at the present time – with the exception of the Bible – is The Pickwick Papers by Charles Dickens. It is largely written in the English of the London streets. Scholars say that, in fifty years' time, the book will be unintelligible to the average reader.

Then Paul goes still further and adds: '*As for knowledge, it will pass away.*'
Where is the wisdom of the ancients? It has vanished completely. Nowadays, a boy at secondary school knows far more than the discoverer of the Law of Gravity, Sir Isaac Newton, knew in his day. The newspaper that brings us the news in the morning is thrown away each night. We can buy encyclopaedias from ten years ago for a few pence, because the scientific discoveries described in their pages are now completely outdated.

The horse-drawn carriage was replaced by steam. And electricity, in turn, is threatening to replace steam, relegating to obscurity hundreds of inventions that have only just been born. One of our greatest living authorities, Sir William Thomson, said at a meeting: 'The steam-engine is passing away.'

'As for knowledge, it will pass away.'

In the back yard of every workshop we see wheels, levers and cranks eaten away by rust. Twenty years ago, those same parts were objects that filled their owner with pride.

Now they represent nothing, apart from a heap of useless old iron.

All the science and philosophy of our day, of which we are so proud, will soon be old.

Some years ago, the greatest figure in Edinburgh was Sir James Simpson, who discovered chloroform, the precursor of anaesthesia. Recently, the university librarian asked the scientist's nephew to pick out the books by his uncle that were no longer of use to the students.

The nephew said to the librarian: 'Take every text-book that is more than ten years old and put it down in the cellar.'

Sir James Simpson was a person of great importance; scientists from all over the world came to consult him.

Meanwhile, his discoveries – and almost all the discoveries of his day – have been consigned to oblivion.

'For now we see in a mirror dimly, but then face to face. Now I know in part; then I shall know fully.'

Can you tell me anything that is going to last for ever? Paul did not bother to name many things. He did not mention money, fortune, fame; he picked out only the things important in his time, the things to which the best men of the day devoted themselves. And he brushed them peremptorily aside.

Paul had nothing against those things in themselves. He does not speak ill of them. He said only that they would not last. They were important things, but they were not supreme gifts.

There were things beyond them.

What we are is more than what we do and far more than what we own. Many things that men call sins are not sins; they are feelings and lapses that will soon disappear.

Ephemeral.

That is a favourite argument of the New Testament. John does not say that the world is wrong; he says that 'it passes away'.

There are many beautiful things in the world, important things that delight and absorb us, but they will not last. Everything in the kingdom of this world – pride and the pleasures of the eye and of the flesh – are here but for a moment.

Therefore, do not love the things of the world. Nothing that the world contains is worth the devotion and time of an immortal soul. The immortal soul should give itself to what is immortal.

And the only immortal things are: Faith, Hope and Love.

Some might say that two of those things also pass away: Faith, when we feel and experience the presence of God, and Hope, when our hopes are fulfilled.

What is certain, though, is that Love will last.

God, the Eternal God, is Love. Therefore seek out Love, that eternal moment, the only thing that will remain when the human race has reached the end of its days. Love will always be the only coinage accepted in the Universe when all the other coinages of all the nations have become useless and valueless.

If you choose to give yourself to many things, give yourself first to Love, and everything else will follow. Give to each thing its proper value.

**G**ive to each thing its proper value. Let the great objective of your lives be to find to find sufficient strength to defend that idea and build a life with Love as its main reference point, as did Christ, who built his whole life around Love.

I said that Love is eternal. Have you ever noticed how often John associates Love with eternal life? When I was a child, I was not told that 'God so loved the world that He gave his only-begotten Son that whosoever believeth in Him should have everlasting life.'

What I was told, I remember, was that God so loved the world that, if we trusted in Him, we would have peace, rest, joy and safety. I had to find out for myself that this wasn't quite true, that all those who trust in Him – that is, all those who love Him, because trust is the only avenue to Love – would have eternal life.

The Gospels speak to us of a new life, therefore do not offer your fellow man only peace, rest, joy and safety. Instead, tell him how Christ came into the world to give us all a life abundant in Love, and therefore abundant in salvation, a life long enough for us to devote ourselves to learning to Love.

That is the only way that the words of the Gospel can make sense and touch body, soul and spirit, and give to each part a goal and an aim.

Many of the spiritual texts we read today are addressed only to one part of our nature.

They offer peace, but do not speak of life.

They discuss Faith and forget about Love.

They talk about justification, not regeneration.

And so we end up drifting away from the spiritual search, because it has failed to keep us on the path.

Let us not make that mistake. Let it be clear that for us only Total Love can compete with the love of the world.

T o love abundantly is to live abundantly. To love for ever is to live for ever. Eternal life is inextricably bound up with Love.

Why do we want to live for ever? Because we hope that tomorrow will bring us someone we can love. Because we want to live another day with the person we love beside us. Because we want to find someone who deserves our Love and who, in turn, will know how to love us as we deserve to be loved.

That is why, when a man has no one to love him, he feels a great desire to die. As long as he has friends, people who love him and whom he loves too, he will live.

Because to live is to love.

Even love for an animal – a dog, for example – can justify the life of a human being. But if he loses that loving bond with life, any reason to go on living will disappear too.

The 'energy of life' will go.

Eternal life means to know Love. God is Love. John says: 'This is life eternal, that they might know Thee the only true God, and Jesus Christ whom Thou hast sent.'

Whatever your belief or faith, first seek out Love. Everything else will follow.

Love is eternal, because God is eternal.

L ove is life.
Love never ends and
life will not end while
there is Love.

That is what Paul is showing us, that, in all created things, Love is present as the Supreme Gift,
because Love remains when all other things pass
away.

Love is here, it exists in us here and now.
It is not something that will be given to us after
we die. On the contrary, we will have very few
chances to learn Love when we are old if we do

not seek it out and practise it now.

No worse fate can befall a man than to live and die alone, unloving and unloved. To love is to be saved.

Not to love or be loved is to be damned.

And he who takes joy in love already takes joy in God, because God is Love.

I have all but finished this very long sermon, but, first, I want to propose something: how many of you would like to join me in reading this part of Paul's Letter to the Corinthians at least once a week for the next three months. A man did that once and it changed his life completely.

Or you could start by reading the letter every day, especially the verses that describe the kind of behaviour that goes with Love:

Love is patient and kind; love does not envy.
Put those ingredients into your life. From then on, everything you do will be eternal. It's worth spending a little time learning the art of Love.

No man becomes a saint in his sleep; he must pray and meditate.

In the same way, any improvement, in any direction, requires preparation and care.

Address yourselves to living a life that is a full and proper one. If you look back, you will see that the best and most important moments of your life were those in which the spirit of Love was present.

When we look at our past – and ignore the transitory pleasures of life – we will see that the important moments of our existence were those in which we experienced Love, unnoticed acts of kindness that we did for those around us, unimportant things sometimes, but which, for a fraction of a second, made us feel as if we had already entered eternal life.

I have seen almost all the beautiful things that God created. I have enjoyed almost all the pleasures a man can experience. However, when I look back at my past, there are only four or five brief moments when I did something that was a poor imitation of God's Love.

Those are the moments that justify my existence. Everything else is transitory. Any other good or virtue is mere illusion. Those small acts of Love that no one noticed, that no one knows about, justify my life.

Because Love endures.

 atthew gives us a classic description of the Final Judgment: the Son of Man is seated upon a throne and, like a shepherd, is dividing the sheep from the goats.

At that moment, the most important question for a human being to ask will not be: 'How did I live?' but 'How did I love?'

The final test of every search for salvation will be Love. What we did or believed or achieved will be of no account.

None of that will count. What will count is how we loved our fellow men and women.

The mistakes we made will not even be remembered. We will be judged by the good we neglected to do, because to keep Love locked up inside us is to go against the spirit of God, it is proof that we never knew Him, that He loved us in vain, and that His Son died in vain.

Not loving means saying that God never inspired our thoughts, our lives, and that we never came close enough to Him to be touched by His exuberant Love. It means:

'I lived for myself, I thought for myself,
For myself and none beside,
Just as if Jesus had never lived,
as if He had never died.'

It is before God that the nations of the world will be reunited. It is in the presence of all men that we will be judged.

And each man will judge himself.

Gathered there together will be those we met and helped. Also present will be those we scorned and denied. There will be no need to call for witnesses, because our own life will be there as evidence of what we did.

No other charge – apart from a lack of Love – will be laid upon us.

Be quite sure, the words we will hear on that day will come not from theology, not from the saints, not from the churches.

They will come from the hungry and from the poor. They will come not from creeds and doctrines.

They will come from the naked and the homeless. They will come not from Bibles and books of prayer.

They will come from the glasses of water that we gave or did not give.

Who is Christ?

He who fed the poor, clothed the naked and visited the sick.

Where is Christ?

'Whoever receives a little child in my name receives me.'

And who is with Christ?

'Whoever loves has been born of God.'

By the time the young man had finished speaking, the sun had already set. The people got up in silence and went to their houses. They would never forget that day for as long as they lived. They had been touched by the Supreme Gift and wanted that afternoon to be remembered for a very long time.

'Although, of course, it will not be remembered for ever,' thought one of them. For as the young man quite rightly said: 'Only Love endures.'

About the author

H enry Drummond was born in Scotland in 1851. When still a young man, he decided to travel the world in search of the meaning of life. Although he had been preaching to small communities since he was twenty-two years old, he systematically refused to enter the clergy, choosing instead to devote himself to teaching natural sciences in Glasgow. *The Greatest Thing in the World*, published in 1890, is his most important work and became known around the world as one of the most beautiful texts ever written about Love.

About Paulo Coelho

P aulo Coelho is considered to be one of the most influential authors of our times. He is also one of the most widely read, and his books have sold more than 195 million copies worldwide, have been published in 170 countries and translated into 80 languages.

He was born in Rio de Janeiro in 1947 and early on discovered his vocation for writing. He has worked as a director, actor and journalist, and his collaboration with Brazilian composer and singer Raul Seixas produced some of Brazil's classic rock songs. In 1986, a crucial meeting led him to make the pilgrimage to Santiago de Compostela. A year later, he wrote *The Pilgrimage*. Then, in 1988, he published *The Alchemist*, the book that would bring him international fame.

Paulo Coelho has written many other books that have touched the hearts of people around the world, among them *Eleven Minutes* – best-selling fiction title worldwide in 2003 – *Veronika Decides to Die*, *The Zahir*, *Aleph*, *Manuscript Found in Accra* and *Adultery*.

He has received numerous prestigious international awards. He has been a member of the Brazilian Academy of Letters since 2002, and in 2007 he was designated as a Messenger of Peace by the United Nations. In 2009 he received the Guinness World Record for the most translated book by a living author (*The Alchemist*).

Paulo is the writer with the highest number of social media followers.

http://paulocoelhoblog.com/

Also by Paulo Coelho

Made in the USA
San Bernardino, CA
25 February 2017

46075104R00068